The Origins of Wisdom

FENG SHUI

O. B. DUANE

First published in Great Britain in 1997 by
Brockhampton Press,
20 Bloomsbury Street,
London WC1B 3QA
A member of the Hodder Headline Group.

ISBN 1 86019 549 0

A copy of the C.I.P. data is available from
the British Library upon request.

Produced for Brockhampton Press by Flame Tree Publishing,
a part of The Foundry Creative Media Company Limited,
The Long House, Antrobus Road, Chiswick, London W4 5HY

The Origins of Wisdom

FENG SHUI

O. B. DUANE

BROCKHAMPTON PRESS

Foreword

꙳

'The Tao is the breath that never dies'

Tao Te Ching

LIVING IN BALANCE with natural forces is a way of living in harmony with the Tao, the flow and order of the universe. From ancient times the Chinese recognized real and imaginary forces alive in the landscape and respected their power and influence. These elements active in the natural and spirit world not only shaped the landscape but also had a profound effect on human fortunes. The skill of Feng Shui practitioners lay in their ability to divine these forces which were at work everywhere and in many forms, particularly in the flow of Chi and the balance of yin and yang.

For centuries Feng Shui has been influential in the lives of the Chinese, from Emperors to ordinary people. Cities were planned according to its laws and the dead buried in the most favourable sites, since the fortune of the dead affected the well being of the living.

During the latter half of the twentieth century interest in Feng Shui has grown rapidly in the West. This book is a useful introduction to the history, philosophy and practice of Feng Shui and gives the reader an interesting insight into this ancient art.

Joanne Robinson, ICOREC, & Zhao Xiaomin
January 1997

The practice of Feng Shui is based on the belief that humans' external surroundings affect their inner happiness.

Contents

According to the principles of Feng Shui, the ideal location of a house's main reception room is on the ground floor.

Introduction

Introduction

This well known word means wind-water,
but its wider sense stands for the relations
to the surrounding nature, the influence of
the landscape on the beauty of the buildings
and the happiness of its inhabitants.

Ernst Börschmann

FENG SHUI IS THE ANCIENT Chinese art of understanding and manipulating the invisible energy of the cosmos, the *Chi*, so that it flows smoothly to create harmony between humans and our environment. The practice of Feng Shui is founded on the belief that the arrangement of our exterior world exerts a powerful influence on our interior equilibrium and personal happiness. The balance of hidden forces in the landscape is maintained when certain laws of object placement and design are adhered to. The *Chi* (the life breath of the universe) which flows along the hidden veins or 'dragon lines' of the earth is both beneficial and harmful. Feng Shui is also a way of understanding the two opposing, yet complementary forces of

The ancient Chinese believed that natural phenomena were occupied by the spirits of tigers and dragons.

龍山和虎谷

yin and *yang,* the watery and the solid, the cool and the hot, the moon and the sun. It is the role of the Feng Shui master (*Hsien-Sheng*) to harness beneficial *Chi* (*Sheng Chi*) and to deflect destructive *Chi* (*Shar Chi*) from a given location, and also to determine the level of *yin* and *yang* in a given place. Good Feng Shui, the pooling of *Sheng Chi*, results in health, wealth, success and stability, whereas bad Feng Shui, the predominance of *Shar Chi*, will lead to illness, unhappiness, accidents and financial loss.

> *The Chinese saw Feng Shui not so much as a superstitious branch by itself of rural practices but an integral part of the study of the land itself and the patterns on it both natural and man-made.*
>
> Stephen Skinner, Feng Shui

Originating in China some five thousand years ago, Feng Shui evolved as the result of a practical need to understand and work with the unpredictable forces of nature, taking into account climate and land, so that good harvests were ensured and favourable settlements established. The ancient Chinese were primarily agricultural people and the early shaman kings of China placed great emphasis on attuning themselves to the laws of nature. Feng Shui may be literally translated as 'wind and water', both of which demonstrate the power of the elements derived from the flow of *Chi*, and the two forces of *yin* and *yang* which shape all life.

My own animal spirits are the animal spirits of my progenitors.
When on my part I carry to the utmost my sincerity and respect
in worshipping them, then the spirits of my ancestors are present
with me. Just like a stalk of grain, when the original plant is dead,
new roots appear on the side — thus connecting the identical real
spirit down from past generations to the present time.

Commentator of the Analects of Confucius

The development of Feng Shui from mythical times through to the rise of the various dynasties before the Han dynasty (206 BC—AD 25) is not well documented. Its historical origins will be looked at in more detail in the chapter to follow, but in tracing its deepest roots, we must turn to the ancient Chinese custom of ancestor worship. According to the nineteenth-century scholar, Ernest Eitel, the 'excessive and superstitious veneration of the spirits of ancestors' is the earliest manifestation of 'the moving spring and leading instinct of the whole Feng Shui system'.[1] Ancient Chinese shamanic religion centred around the notion of a powerful spirit world occupying natural phenomena, which should be treated with the utmost respect. As a result of this belief, the tombs of the dead were carefully chosen and a favourable site with a strong flow of *Chi* was thought to bestow good fortune upon all the descendants of the deceased.

Overleaf: *Feng Shui teaches that opposites, such as fire and water, can complement each other to create harmony.*

Over the centuries, Feng Shui has evolved into a highly complex art. It is intrinsically linked to traditional Taoist philosophy, which looked upon the Tao, the way of the universe, as the architect of essential laws, yet enriched by folklore, mystical beliefs, metaphysics, mathematics and astrology. Its rapid increase in popularity from the Han dynasty onwards led Feng Shui masters to be consulted on everything, from the best site for an imperial residence or grave to the fortunes of individuals and the proper arrangement of furniture inside the home.

The art of Feng Shui reached its peak during the Sung dynasty which finally fell in AD1279. It experienced something of a resurgence during the Ching Dynasty (AD 1644—1911), but with the end of the dynastic era and the rise of communism Feng Shui suffered a substantial decline in mainland China. In Taiwan, Hong Kong and Singapore, however, its influence has never deteriorated, and it is an extremely important part of everyday life in those countries, infiltrating both private and business worlds. There has also been a marked increase in the popularity of Feng Shui in the West over the past ten years and many people have incorporated its philosophies and methods into their working environment and personal lives with a view to promoting harmony and good fortune.

Author's Note

This book is intended as an introduction only to the ancient art of Feng Shui: it does not aim to instruct the reader in its practice, nor is it by any means an exhaustive study. Readers wishing to explore this subject in greater depth should refer to the list of Suggested Further Reading.

[1]   Eitel, Ernest J., *Feng-Shui, the Science of Sacred Landscape in Old China.*

Chi flows along the hidden veins or 'dragon lines' of the earth and can be both beneficial and harmful.

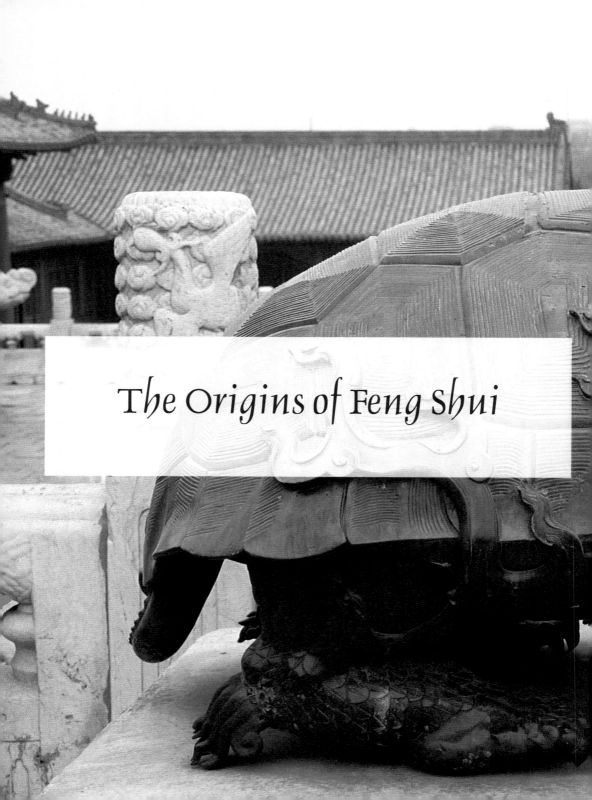

The Origins of Feng Shui

The Origins of Feng Shui

Historical Background

ACCORDING TO CHINESE TRADITION, it was Fu Xi, the first legendary ruler of China, who gained knowledge of the influences of cosmic forces upon the earth. Legend has it that a great dragon-horse emerged from the River Ho, revealing on its back the original eight trigrams — geometric patterns composed of three lines each, explaining the mysteries of heaven and earth, also known as the *Ho-t'u*. Having studied these diagrams which appeared in a sequence known as the Former Heaven sequence, Fu Xi became highly skilled in the art of divination and acquired insight into the fundamental structure of the universe and the waxing and waning of the cosmic *yin* and *yang*.

Two more legendary figures are also associated with the early development of Feng Shui. The first, Huang Ti, or Yellow Emperor, who is said to have lived around 2700 BC, is credited with the invention of the compass and the first calendar, tools which became central to the practice of Feng Shui. Slightly later, around 2205 BC, Yü, the founder of the Xia dynasty, is reputed to have witnessed a turtle emerge from the River Lo with the numbers and grid pattern of the *Lo-shu* magical square inscribed on its back. With the help of this square, it is said that Yü arrived at a more practical understanding of the universe rooted in his more immediate surroundings. Both the trigrams and the *Lo-shu* square are discussed in greater detail in the chapter to follow.

The correct equilibrium must be found between all things before contentment and harmony can be established.

Imperial Cloisonne Plaque

The cycle has turned into a new year with all its splendour,
The beginning of Spring occuring in the first month;
The Hundred Creatures in harmony with the Seven Musics,
And myriad happiness come in pairs.

The Five Planets meet with Yingshi
The Three Ranks ascend to the Eastern Hall;
Zhuanxu starts the first rhythm.
Watching the hours we exert ourselves in our duties.

Seeing off the cold the day forebodes good fortune,
We foster things in accordance with the seasons and work hard;
The Su poetry and the Xin songs,
One could easily be misled to consider them facile.

The words above are those featured on the plaque opposite.

From the original eight trigrams of Fu Xi, a new sequence known as the Later Heaven sequence was created, followed by the sixty-four hexagrams. This work is said to have been undertaken by King Wên, the first ruler of the Zhou dynasty (1121—255 BC) who, during a period of imprisonment before his rise to power, set about rearranging the Former Heaven sequence and exploring all possible combinations of the eight trigrams of the Later Heaven Sequence with a view to explaining the whole scheme of heaven and earth pervaded by *yin* and *yang*. It was these sixty-four hexagrams, together with short commentaries for correct conduct and ethical standards that eventually formed the *I Ching (Book of Changes)*, a work containing the fundamental building blocks of the system of Feng Shui. King Wên's original manuscript, known as the *Chou-i*, has long since disappeared and the *I Ching*, as it has been passed on to us today, is based on fragments of the old text on which Confucius worked for much of his later life.

A great man at work accords with heaven and so his influence spreads everywhere. As water flows to what is wet and fire turns to what is dry so, by inner affinity, what is born of heaven accords with what is above: what is born of earth with what is below. Each follows its own kind. To follow the great man: therein is blessing.

I Ching (Book of Changes)

Ancient Feng Shui masters would pass their knowledge on orally to a few select scholars.

Under the direction of King Wên's grandson, Emperor Shing, the practical application of the theories set forth in the *Chou-i* were encouraged. The compass was improved upon and the calendar further revised. During the Shang dynasty (1766—1121 BC) units of time and place, the Ten Celestial Stems and the Twelve Terrestrial Branches, were introduced to the calendar and a sixty-day/sixty-year cycle established. By the third century BC, the time of the Han dynasty, the Ten Celestial Stems had been divided into five couplets and matched with five terrestrial elements — earth, fire, water, metal and wood, and the five planets — Venus, Jupiter, Mercury, Mars and Saturn.[1] The Twelve Terrestrial Branches were made to signify the twelve months of the year, the twelve double hours of the day, the twelve points of the Chinese compass and the twelve animals of the Chinese horoscope. In assessing a site, the ancient Chinese considered it essential to take an individual's birth-date into account since they believed that man's fate was influenced by the astrological predictions of the year of birth.

It was during the Han dynasty that the *fang-shih*, practitioners of the arts of divination, emerged as an important group, exerting a powerful influence on social and political life. One of these practitioners, who is mentioned in historical records of that period, was known as Zhang Liang. A brilliant scholar and military strategist, Zhang Liang is reputed to have engineered the fall of the tyrannical Chin dynasty (255—206 BC).[2] His military success was attributed to his skill in divining the manoeuvres of his enemies, part of the great art of divination he had studied under two powerful masters, Chih-sun Tzu (Red Pine Master) and Huang Shih-kung (Yellow Stone Master). It is said that the Yellow Stone Master was the first to promote Feng Shui among the common people, since he began a tradition of training talented disciples to spread its philosophies throughout the land.

Chinese burial sites are considered female (yin), and houses of the living are thought to be male (yang).

The Literature of Feng Shui

As the Han dynasty progressed, Feng Shui, or *K-an-yu* as it was then called, became a professional skill and the first attempts were now made to document popular reactions and beliefs in order to form them into some sort of system. Fragments of records have been unearthed by archaeologists, containing indirect references to Feng Shui dating from the third or fourth centuries BC. It is generally assumed, however, that up until the rise of the Han dynasty, masters passed on their knowledge orally to a select few, fearful of sharing it with ordinary scholars, critics and the ruling classes.

Only the titles of the earliest books have survived, but their existence is supported in the historical records of subsequent dynasties. The *Tseh-Ching* (*The Cannon of the Dwellings*) is said to have appeared during the Han dynasty, a book Eitel describes as 'not only a condensation of the geomantic superstitions of former ages', but one which also carried 'the doctrine of Feng Shui farther by extending the geomantic influences, which were formerly ascribed to graves only, to the dwellings of the living.' Burial sites were now considered female (*yin*), while the houses of the living were considered male (*yang*). The book also divided King Wên's eight trigrams into either male or female so that both graves and dwelling houses could be more suitably chosen.

The next important work to emerge on the art of Feng Shui was written during the Chin dynasty (AD 265—420) by a Taoist scholar known as Kuo-p'u. Often described as the modern founder of Feng Shui, Kuo-p'u was an expert in tomb orientation and in the general evaluation of nature's forms and outlines. His two classics, *Ch'uang-shu* (*The Book of Burials*), and *Ch'ing-lung-Ching* (*Book of Landscapes*) gathered together all the ancient traditions of Feng Shui. Both texts are first mentioned in the catalogue of the later Tang dynasty (AD 618—906).

If all things do not have a void in the centre, if they do not have form as substance, if yin does not have yang, how can they come into existence? Know the light and hold on to the dark. This is the secret of being. Those who know this intuitively know the wondrous way of the Tao.

Kuo-p'u, Ch'ing-lung-Ching

During the Tang dynasty, a period which offered a highly favourable climate to the evolution of the arts and sciences in general, the *K-an-yu* as practised by Kuo-p'u was more properly established as a branch of Taoist knowledge. His work was then continued by other influential scholars, and at this time quite a large number of writings on the subject of Feng Shui emerged.

The most important of all the Tang masters was Yang Yun-Sung, an enthusiastic supporter of Kuo-p'u and principal advisor to the Emperor, who is said to have written three very significant texts — the *Han-Lung-Ching (The Canon on the Art of Rousing the Dragon)* the *Ch'ing-Nang Ao-Chih (The Canon of the Secret Meanings of the Universe)* and the *I-Lung-Ching (The Canon for the Approximation of the Dragon)*. Yang Yun-Sung is credited above all with developing the theories of the Form School of Feng Shui, which placed great emphasis on the shapes of the mountains, the direction of watercourses and the position of the lair of the dragon using the compass only as a subordinate help in determining the most auspicious site.

Overleaf: *The theories of the Form School emphasized the position of the lair of the dragon when selecting building sites.*

Many other minor schools of Feng Shui flourished during the Tang era, all starting out with the same fundamental mythological and cosmological theories, yet interpreted differently according to individual preference. Some practitioners placed great emphasis on the use of the geomancer's compass, the *lo-p'an*. Others developed a whole theory on the influence of the various constellations and their interaction with the points of the compass, while yet others concentrated exclusively on the shape of the landscape as a focus of divination.

By the rise of the Sung dynasty (AD 960) several more great masters had appeared. At this time the art of Feng Shui was developed more methodically and metaphysical theories applied to it. A second major school now arose known as the Compass School, which emphasized, in particular, the importance of the eight trigrams, the Celestial Stems and Terrestrial Branches and the arrangement of the constellations, assigning only minor importance to the configurations of the landscape. Its chief exponent was a scholar known as Wang Chih, who is said to have invented the theory of the mutual production and destruction of the Five Elements.

In the Form School the principles are clear but the practice is difficult ... with the Compass the principles are obscure but the practice is easy.

Chao Fang, Tsang shu wen ta

Ursa Major, also known as the Great Bear, was one of the constellations studied by the Compass School.

Ursa Major (The Great Bear)

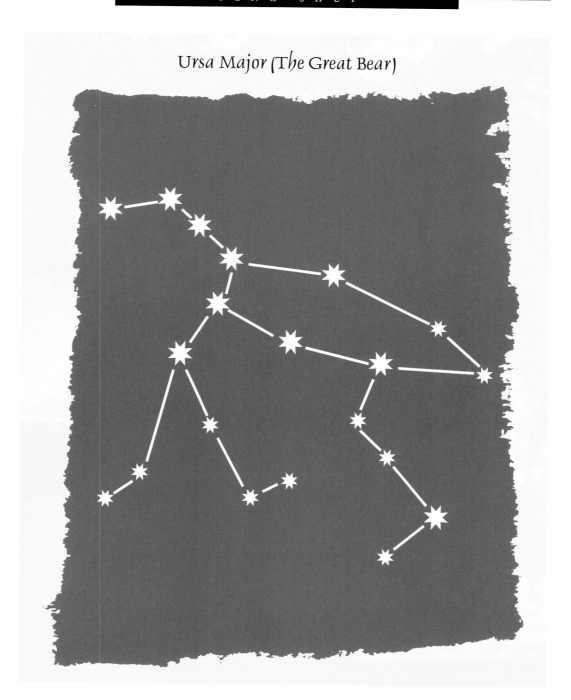

By the time of the Southern Sung dynasty (AD 1127—1279), Feng Shui had become a systematic science and its masters were much revered throughout society. Less than a century later, however, this state of affairs was reversed as the Ming Emperor, Zhu Yüan-Zhang, began purging the land of all political competitors. His former military advisor, the Taoist master of the divination arts, Liu Po-hun, was one such target, and, as an extension of the Emperor's political policy, it followed that all Taoist practitioners of the divination arts suffered his persecution. A professional class of Feng Shui practitioners therefore replaced the old Taoist masters, as a result of which the art became increasingly separated from Taoist philosophies. Some attempts were made during the Ching dynasty (AD 1644—1911) to redress this situation and much criticism was levelled at those who had adulterated the practice by rejecting the wisdom and sophistication of the Sung theorists in favour of commercial success.

During the nineteenth century, the divide between the two main schools of Feng Shui, the Form School and the Compass School, was much less pronounced. Practitioners used a combination of theories and practices drawn from both schools and few regarded Feng Shui as a purely Taoist art. Modern Feng Shui is resonant of ancient Taoist philosophies, but it has evolved into a profession, and one by which one may earn a living. Consultants nowadays perform a variety of commercial tasks, from choosing an office site, to designing a house interior, to improving the marital relations or general well-being of their clients.

[1]   The ancient Chinese did not acknowledge the existence of Pluto.
[2]   There were two Chin dynasties, the first, 255—206 BC, the second, 265—420 AD.

The Hanging Temple evokes a time when Feng Shui principles were inseparable from Taoism.
During Emperor Zhu Yuan-Zhang's persecution of Taoists, Feng Shui became a separate movement.

Fundamental Principles

禄

後有不忘永継承

公元一九九四年歲甲戌正月上浣 口

光前

宗功祖德流芳里

孝 愕
女 禄仲輝
渭嘉
舆慧 从孫
男 聰健

福

Fundamental Principles

Feng Shui — wind and water, the outward and
visible signs of celestial yang and yin; the art of
adapting the residence of the living and the dead
so as to harmonize with the cosmic breath.

The Encyclopedia Sinica

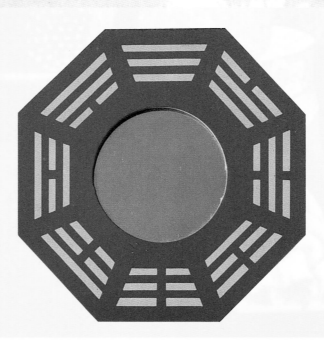

THE CHIEF GOAL OF THE FENG SHUI practitioner is to achieve the balance and harmony between *yin* and *yang* and the divine flow of the cosmic breath, whether of landscape, house or building. Whatever method he or she may choose, there are certain basic principles and procedures rooted in history and tradition common to every practice.

The Tao and the Chi

The ancient Chinese held the belief that from the Supreme Ultimate, the Tao, or *Li*, issued the life force of the universe, the *Chi*. The Tao is the Way, the harmonious way of the universe, which has no form or shape or dimension. Yet it contains within its breath the opposing forces of *yin* and *yang* upon which the correct balance of all things depends. The relationship between the *Li* and the *Chi* is best explained in the words of the ancient philosopher, Chu Xi:

Throughout heaven and earth there is Li and there is Chi. Li is the Tao [organizing] all forms from above, and the root from which all things are produced. Chi is the instrument [composing] all forms from below, and the tools and raw materials with which all things are made. Thus men and all other things must receive this Li at the moment of their coming into being, and thus get their specific nature; so also must they receive this Chi and thus get their form.

Chu Xi

Opposite: The eight trigrams indicate the four cardinal points and the four sub-directions of the compass.

Yin and Yang — (T'ai-Chi)

Yin and Yang are opposing forces, but each must interact, and each contain an element of the other, in order to produce harmony.

Yin and Yang — (T'ai-Chi)

The terms *yin* and *yang* were first used in the *I Ching (Book of Changes)* and they signify the dualism of all creation and the flux of the universe. Although they are opposing forces, they must always interact to produce harmony, and within each there should always be an element of the other. This explains why there is always a circle of white within the dark *yin* and a circle of black within the white *yang*. *Yang* is light and *yin* is dark and the two are represented in the *I Ching* as a continuous line (▬▬▬▬) *(yang)* and a broken line (▬▬ ▬▬) *(yin)*.

The Receptive, the primal Yin nature, is the complement, not the opposite, of The Creative. It does not combat The Creative but completes it. It is earth as against heaven; nature as against spirit; wife as against husband; son as against father or an official as against his ruler.

I Ching (Book of Changes)

As far as Feng Shui is concerned, *yin* and *yang* have different attributes and are made to symbolize various aspects of the universe. For example, *yang*, the Creative male principle, is associated with the South, light, sun, summer, Heaven, mountains, the dragon, and even numbers. *Yin*, the Receptive female principle, is associated with the North, moon, cold, wet, dark, winter, lowlands, the tiger and all the odd numbers.

The Pa Kua (Eight Trigrams)

From the basic *yin* and *yang* symbols (broken line and continuous line), eight trigrams were produced indicating the four cardinal points around the compass and the four sub-directions. The centre is also regarded as one of the compass points. They were conceived as images of everything that was happening in heaven and earth and came to be associated with the Five Elements, the seasons, various colours, and certain characteristics and attributes. When arranged around an octagonal symbol known as the *Pa Kua* these trigrams served as one of the most important tools of the Feng Shui practitioner.

Former Heaven

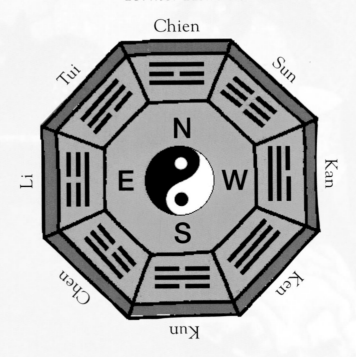

Nowadays, the Former Heaven arrangement discovered by Fu Xi is reproduced on mirrors as protection against malevolent spirits or the predominance of *Shar Chi*. It is also used in the upkeep of ancestral *yin* burial sites where redesign is required. The Later Heaven arrangement is more pragmatically applied to the *yang* dwellings of the living and is the one most used in modern practice. It should be noted that the Chinese compass is the opposite way round to a Western compass, with south at the top, north at the bottom, west to the right and east to the left.

Later Heaven

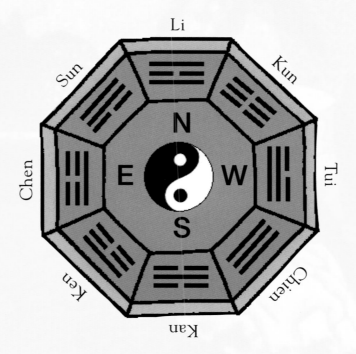

The Former Heaven arrangement is used in the upkeep of burial sites, while the Later Heaven is applied to the houses of the living.

The Eight Trigrams and Their Attributes

This is the Later Heaven Sequence, moving clockwise from *Li* in the South

Trigram	Emblem	Element	Direction	Season	Colour	Image
Li *The Clinging*	Lightning	Fire	South	Summer	Red	Weapons/ Sunshine/ Drought
Kun *The Receptive*	Earth	Earth	Southwest	Late Summer Early Autumn	Beige/ Yellow	Nourishment/ Devotion
Tui *The Lake*	Lake	Water/ Metal	West	Mid-Autumn	White/ Silver/ Gold	Mirrors/ Reflections
Chien *The Creative*	Heaven	Metal	Northwest	Late Autumn	White/ Silver/ Gold	Strength/ Energy
Kan *The Danger*	Moon/ Water	Water	North	Mid-Winter	Black/ Blue	Wheels/ Curves/Mental disturbance/ Danger

Trigram	Emblem	Element	Direction	Season	Colour	Image
☶						
Ken	Mountain	Wood	Northeast	Early Spring	Beige	Gates/ fruits
The Stillness						Seeds
☳						
Chen	Thunder	Wood	East	Spring	Green/	Movement/roads
The Arousing					Brown	Bamboo sprouts
☴						
Sun	Wind	Wood	Southeast	Late Spring	Green	Plants/Growth
The Wind				Early Summer		

There are also eight 'enrichments', eight numbers and eight colours associated with the eight directions of the *Pa Kua* as follows:

South *(Li)*   Prosperity and recognition (purple, 9)
Southwest *(Kun)*   Marital happiness and peace (black, 2)
West *(Tui)*   Fertility and pleasure (red, 7)
Northwest *(Chien)*   New beginnings (white, 6)
North *(Kan)*   Success (white, 1)
Northeast *(Ken)*   Children and family (white, 8)
East *(Chen)*   Wisdom and experience (blue, 3)
Southeast *(Sun)*   Wealth and prosperity (green, 4)

Overleaf: *Mountains and hills have great significance in the practice of Feng Shui, in landscape they are represented by the Black Tortoise.*

Within the mountains: heaven. Hidden riches.
So the wise man studies the sayings of old
And the deeds of the past to enrich himself.

I Ching (Book of Changes)

The Lo-shu Magical Square

The *Lo-shu* magical square is a very ancient device reputedly discovered by Emperor Yü of the Xia dynasty. This traditional three-by-three grid has been used by Chinese geomancers over the centuries, particularly those of the Compass School, in the building of cities, imperial palaces, temples and mansions which were traditionally divided into nine sectors. It has been asserted that in feudal times the landowner who could afford to build a house with nine rooms circulated from room to room according to the season of the year in order that he might rule wisely over his subjects.

The *Lo-shu* square is divided into equally sized smaller squares numbered one to nine which are also sometimes referred to as the Nine Palaces. The sequence of the numbers corresponds to the Later Heaven sequence of the eight trigrams (5). The odd numbers (*yin*) form the four cardinal points of the square and the centre of the square, while the even numbers (*yang*) form the inter-cardinal points. The numbers, when added up either diagonally or in rows, always add up to fifteen, which is the number of days it takes for a new moon to become a full moon.

The Lo Shu Magical Square is used as a guide in the building of cities, temples and mansions.

When followed in a clockwork direction the numbers indicate the flow of the *yin* and the *yang* throughout the annual cycle. Each of the trigrams, as we have already seen, is associated with a season, an element and a compass direction. South, therefore, is always associated with the summer, with fire, and the number 9, whereas north is always associated with winter, with water and the number 1. The numbers of the *Lo-shu* square give added meaning to the trigrams and when the grid is used in conjunction with the *Pa Kua* using the compass direction as a guide, it allows the Feng Shui practitioner to identify good sectors according to seasonal fluctuations and also helps to neutralize bad ones.

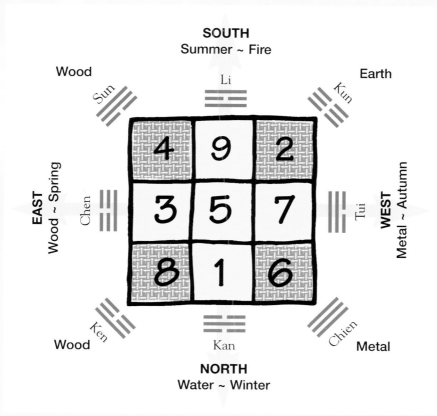

The Numbers and Their Associations

1 One represents the ultimate. It is the number of the gods, but mortals cannot occupy this position comfortably for too long.

2 Two is a happy number representing the balance of the *yin-yang* forces.

3 Three is the number of visual stability and unity.

4 Four has the most unpleasant association of all the numbers and represents death.

5 Five is the most auspicious number representing power and good fortune.

6 Six is a good number for neutralizing a troublesome area.

7 Seven confers magic power.

8 Eight symbolizes harmony and happiness and also has religious associations.

9 Nine is a very positive number and is associated with long life and happiness.

Fire and water are opposites by nature,
So a wise man differentiates with care.
He separates things in order to unite them,
That each should find its proper place.

I Ching (Book of Changes)

The Five Elements

The chart on pages 48-49 reveals the relation of the trigrams to the seasons, directions, colours and the Five Elements. Above all else, the ancient Chinese were careful not to interfere with the order of nature, for they believed that misfortune often arose from disturbances of the Five Elements and acknowledged both a productive and a destructive cycle of these elements. They believed, for example, that it was beneficial to place objects together where they complemented each other. Wood feeds fire, fire feeds the earth, earth gives birth to metal, metal strengthens water, and water creates wood. This is a nourishing and productive cycle. But it becomes destructive and counteractive if wood dominates earth, earth obstructs water, water puts out fire, fire melts metal, and metal breaks wood.

The Productive Cycle   The Destructive Cycle

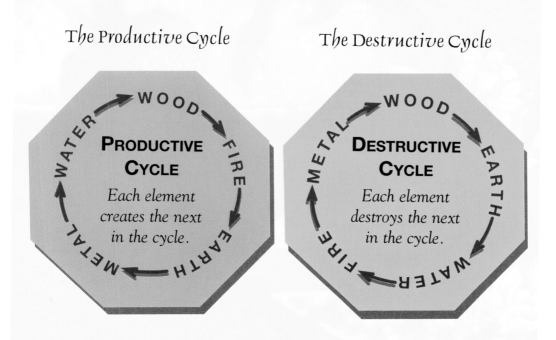

The Chinese believe that the Five Elements relate to each other in two cycles of creation and destruction.

The Four Animals

The Form School of Feng Shui, whose founder was Yang Yun-Sung, placed great emphasis on the shapes of the mountains, the direction of watercourses and the position of the lair of the dragon, using the compass only as a subordinate help in determining the most auspicious site. His theories have been incorporated in particular into the modern practice of exterior Feng Shui, where a site for a house or any other building is required. The dragon, the tiger, the phoenix and the turtle are symbols of the forces of nature and each has its own mythology and characteristics and its own element. Each one is applied to the four principal directions of the Chinese compass.

If a human ruler likes to destroy eggs and nests, the phoenix will not rise. If he likes to drain the waters and take out all the fishes, the dragon will not come. If he likes to kill pregnant animals and murder their young, the unicorn will not appear. If he likes stopping the watercourses and filling up the valleys, the tortoise will not show itself.

Ta Tai Li Chi

The Four Animals — dragon, tiger, phoenix and turtle — symbolize the forces of nature.

The Dragon

The azure dragon is male (*yang*), its element is wood and it must always be to the left (east). In exterior Feng Shui he is found in raised land — a mountain range or a steep hill. Indoors, he might be represented by a solid wall offering shelter from the elements. The dragon is protective and should always appear with the complementary white tiger.

The Tiger

The white tiger is female (*yin*) and is always to the right (west). She is said to represent earth and is found in the lowlands, valleys and river banks. The dragon must always be in a higher place than the white tiger who should never dominate. If there is a mountain to the west of a site and flatter land to the east, for example, this does not present a favourable location, since the white tiger will prove too strong for the azure dragon. The white tiger is also associated with water and it is good to have a lake, pond, stream or even an aquarium in this region.

Red Bird

To the south is the realm of the red phoenix representing the *yang* force — summer, light, prosperity — and, as such, is the most auspicious direction of the compass. In ancient China all temples and other important structures faced southwards.

Black Tortoise

To the rear of any site, which should face north, the *yin* force of the black tortoise dominates. He is represented by a range of hills protecting the site from the chill north winds. The main entrance of a house should never face north and it is preferable to have a solid, heavy wall in place of windows or doors.

The Four Animals must be represented in the landscape in the correct attitude.

The Luo'pan

The *Luo'pan* is the instrument used by the Feng Shui practitioner to determine the most favourable orientation of a building and the correct arrangement of its interior contents and architectural features. There are several types of *Luo'pan* available, some more complicated than others, and there are also varying degrees of usage, depending on the methods of the Feng Shui practitioner. The compass is circular in shape with a diameter ranging from six to eight inches. It is usually made of a tough, lacquered wood set into a metal casing. At the centre of the circle is a small mariner's compass with a magnetic needle painted half red (indicating south) and half black (indicating north).

The number of rings surrounding the central compass may vary from a simple nine-ringed design to a thirty-six-ringed design. Each of the rings contains symbols and information which allow for an accurate reading of a site when interpreted in conjunction with the horoscope of the individual concerned. The most important rings for the modern practitioner are: the Twenty-four Directions Circle (generally known as the twenty-four mountains) describing the physical features of the immediate environment; the Former Heaven Circle, describing the fixed force of the universe, the Tao; and the Later Heaven Circle, describing the eight trigrams used in *I Ching* divination. Other circles contain the symbols of the Ten Celestial Stems and the Twelve Terrestrial Branches, the Five Elements, the sixty-four hexagrams and the twenty-four phases of the solar calendar.

Opposite: The Luo'pan, or Geomancer's Compass, is used to ascertain the most favourable arrangement of a building and its contents.
Overleaf: The dimensions of a building are very important in achieving the correct flow of Chi throughout.

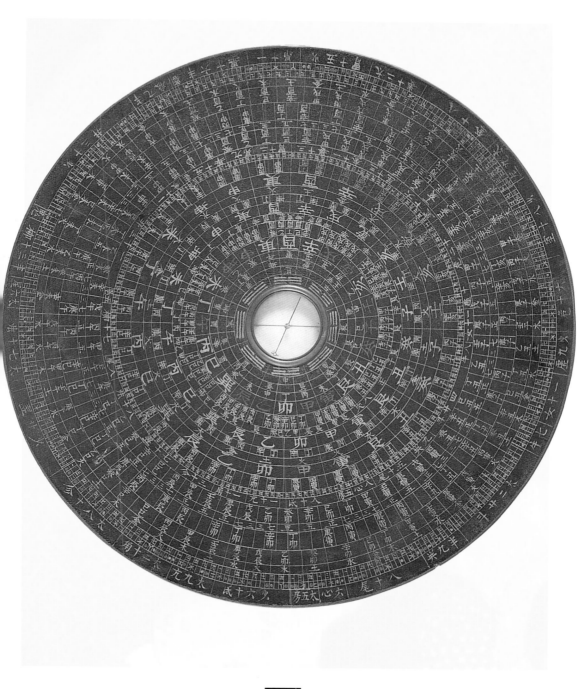

The Geomancer's Ruler

本	害	劫	官	義	離	病	財
興旺 進寶 登科 財至	口舌 病臨 死謎 災至	財失 離鄉 退口	官置 憂置 橫財 順科	大吉 富子 益財 旅丁	失脱 官鬼 劫財 無庚	疾等 爭執 公事 退財	迎福 六合 富貴 財傑

The art of Feng Shui also emphasizes the importance of a building's dimensions and these are carefully checked to ensure good fortune and prosperity. The geomancer's ruler measures exactly 43 cm x 5 cm and is divided into two lines for both external and internal use, with thirty-two parts on the external line below the inch markings, and forty on the internal line above the centimetre markings. Each group of four boxes represents alternately either good fortune or bad luck. For example, the first four boxes on the external line reading from right to left are known as *cai*, or prosperity, while the second group is known as *bing*, and represents illness and misfortune. There is also a character written in the middle of each group of four denoting the general fortune for each group.

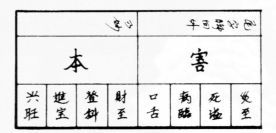

本				害			
興旺	進寶	登科	財至	口舌	病臨	死謎	災至

Above and detail: The Geomancer's Ruler measures the dimensions of a building, determining whether they are good and bad.
Opposite: When the eight trigrams are arranged around a Pa Kua, they are one of a Feng Shui practitioner's most important tools.

Practical Remedies

Practical Remedies

Within the earth a mountain. Inner wealth.
Thus, the wise ruler reduces fullness
And augments that which is too little.
He weighs things and makes them equable.

I Ching (Book of Changes)

EXPLORED VERY BRIEFLY in this section are some of the practical suggestions a modern Feng Shui practitioner might make if consulted on the choice of home or business premises and the arrangement of their interiors.

Feng Shui and the Home

If you are choosing a site on which to build a house, it is most important to take into account the natural features of the landscape. If you are buying a home that is already built in a city or busy town you must be aware of the surrounding buildings and compensate for the absence of natural forms. Houses built alongside one another, for example, should follow a regular pattern enabling the Chi to flow evenly and smoothly. You should also try to ensure that your house is not over-

Opposite: *Evergreen trees positioned near to a house,*
will bring particularly good fortune and are a source of yang.
Overleaf: *The land in front of a house should be open and ideally contain a water source.*

shadowed by a taller structure. A taller house behind you will offer protection, but if positioned directly opposite, the flow of Chi may be seriously inhibited. Where there is no access to a natural water source, a pond before the main entrance will help to establish the balance of yin and yang.

The four animals, representing the four cardinal directions of the compass, have already been mentioned in the previous chapter and they are symbolic guides to the most favourable locations. Mountain ranges or steep hills must be to the east, at the left of the house, and to the north, at the back of the house. Where mountains are not a feature of the land, trees will function in the same way. Evergreen trees will bring particularly good fortune and are a source of *yang*. The front door should welcome the summer (south) and the land in front of the house should be open and ideally contain a water source – a small river or stream – to induce the flow of *Sheng Chi*. The front garden should slope downwards from the main entrance so that it is at a lower level than the back of the house. It should also be smaller and narrower than the back garden since this will channel more energy into the protective sector at the rear resulting in prosperity for the household. Wind directions are also important. No house should be built on flat land entirely exposed to the elements as this will cause the *Chi* to be scattered. Sites that offer shelter from the prevailing winds are the most desirable.

The great man perpetuates his brightness
And illumines all quarters of the world.

I Ching (Book of Changes)

Art and its position in the home is important in Feng Shui, for instance a cold, north-facing wall can be enlivened by paintings in warm colours.

The House Interior

Some basic rules should always be applied to the three most important rooms of the house, namely the main reception room, or sitting-room, the kitchen, and the master bedroom.

Main Reception Room

The main reception room should ideally be situated on the ground floor. It should have good natural light and be spacious and uncluttered. Protruding corners or sharp intersections are a bad omen and should be neutralized as much as possible by using a trailing plant or subtle lighting effects. Overhead beams or columns which dominate a room are considered very inauspicious. In the case of an overhead beam, it is advisable to have a false ceiling installed, but if this is not feasible, furniture should certainly be rearranged so that family members or guests are not forced to sit directly underneath a beam. Columns may be camouflaged by a large plant or they may be encased in floor-to-ceiling mirrors.

The Kitchen

Kitchen design is very important in Feng Shui, since this room directly affects the well-being of all those people living in the house. It should be square or rectangular in shape and should never be located at the very centre of the house where strong cooking smells can travel into other rooms. The kitchen door should not face the front entrance or the back exit, since good luck can easily seep outdoors in this way. Similarly, it should never be positioned next to the bathroom allowing the circulation of germs. The best location for a kitchen, according to the *Yang Dwelling Classic* is in the south, the focus of *yang* energy and the quarter associated with the element of fire.

Opposite: Inauspicious columns in a room can be hidden by mirrors or plants.
Overleaf: The main reception room should be spacious and uncluttered.

The Master Bedroom

Ideally, the master bedroom should be rectangular in shape. An L-shaped bedroom is considered particularly inauspicious. The bed should never face the entrance, since this will drain away energy, nor should the room face on to a stairway allowing destructive energy to rush straight in. It is advisable also to have no more than one doorway in the bedroom. Objects should not be stored underneath the bed as this may lead to ill-health, and there should be no exposed beams in the room since they will result in restless nights.

Feng Shui and Business

A significant number of business premises worldwide have been built according to the laws of Feng Shui, including the Hong Kong and Shanghai Bank in the Orient, and the Shell building and Citibank in the West.

A business premises should be sited on a road where traffic is slow-moving and, if possible, there should be some sort of open space, a park or public garden, in front of the structure. The building should never be hemmed in and those which face a cross-roads or are close to flyovers are considered very unlucky. Again, following the four animals principle, buildings to the left should be higher than buildings to the right.

It is considered good Feng Shui to position a fountain either inside or outside an office building. An aquarium containing goldfish is also a good way to ward off negative influences and promote healthy profits. The foyer should be large and airy, since this area functions as a collection point of benevolent energy and a buffer against malevolent energy. Within the offices themselves, desks should never be placed directly beneath structural beams, but should ideally be located against a wall offering support and protection.

The Hong Kong and Shanghai Bank in the Orient is built according to the principles of Feng Shui..

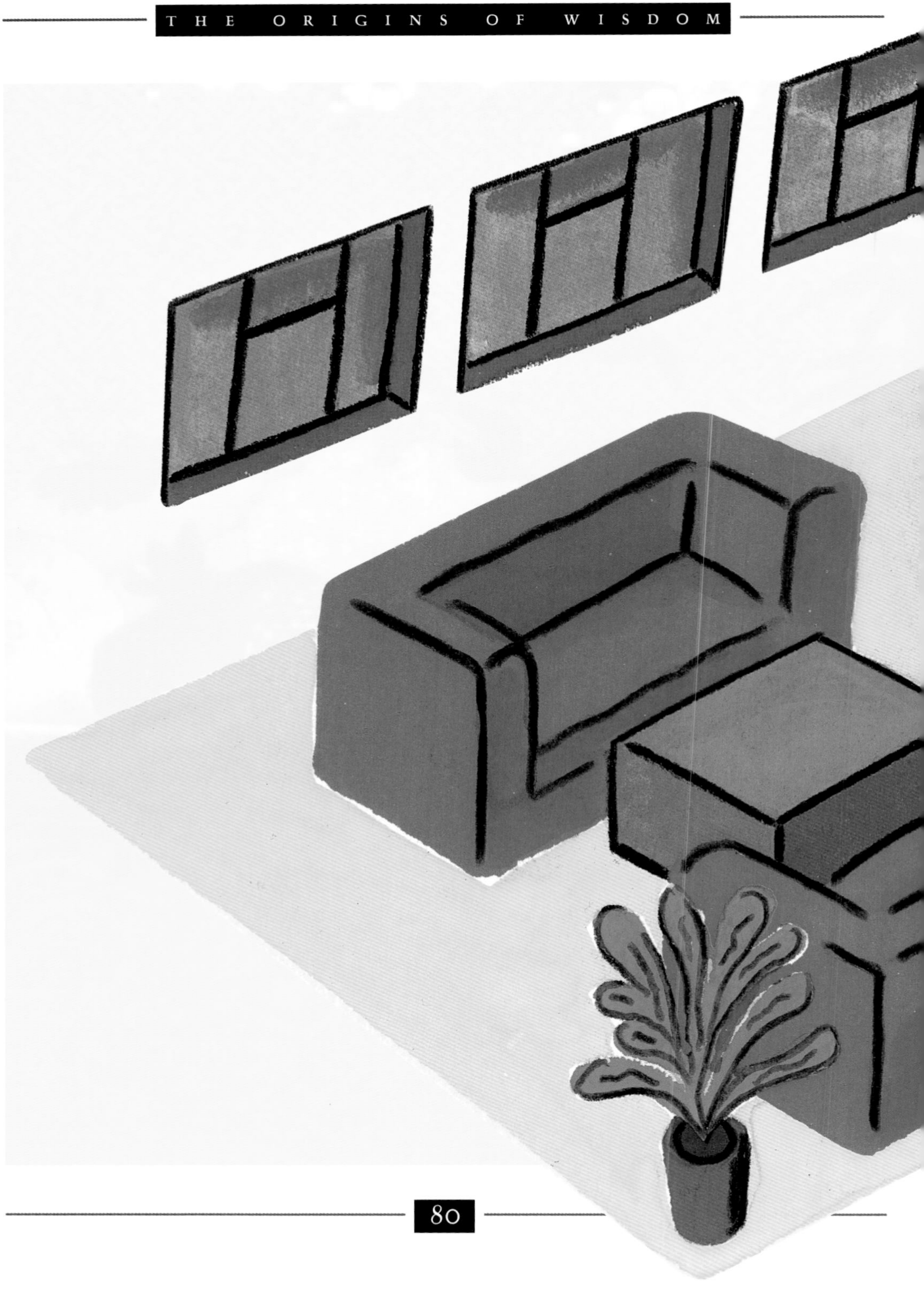

A Feng Shui office interior, with desks, chairs,
doors and windows in the most auspicious places.

If purchasing a retail unit, do not choose one at a lower level than the neighbouring building or good fortune will drain away. Avoid pointed roofs and glass windows which occupy the entire front, since these will bring misfortune. An awning will provide shelter against negative energy and prevent positive energy from leaking out.

Remedies for Bad Feng Shui

A number of simple devices or 'enhancers' are used in Feng Shui to counter bad influences and encourage positive ones. The most important of these and their significance are as follows:

Mirrors: when strategically placed, mirrors can reflect *Shar Chi* out of a building and encourage *Sheng Chi* to establish itself by capturing good light or a positive view or image. Any bright reflective objects, such as lights or rock crystal, will function in the same way.

Life: a living plant will stimulate the flow of *Sheng Chi* and larger plants can be used to regulate the flow of *Chi* where it is travelling too fast.

Sound: wind chimes and bells are commonly used in Feng Shui arrangements to attract good luck. Melodic noises are thought to stimulate the flow of stagnant *Chi*. Audio equipment such as radio, television or stereo, at an appropriate sound level, will also renew the flow.

Opposite: A living plant stimulates the flow of Sheng Chi, as does a small river or stream.
Overleaf: Objects which have a circular motion, such as windmills, stimulate the correct flow of Chi.

Movement: objects which have a circular motion — overhead fans, mobiles — or objects which use natural wind power — windmills, weathervanes — are used to either stimulate or deflect *Chi* under the direction of a Feng Shui consultant.

Art: paintings with warm colours will add life to a cold north-facing wall. A canvas depicting a lake or river is well situated on a west wall, the home of the white tiger.

Colour: colours are closely related to the compass directions and to the Five Elements (see page 55). When used in harmony they order the forces of *yin* and *yang*.

Jade: the ancient Chinese considered jade to be a very sacred stone, a gift from the gods to mankind below. For this reason, small pieces of jade or small carved statues are often used to combat unfavourable forces.

*Opposite: Jade is considered to be a gift
to mankind from the gods, and is thus often used to combat negative forces.*
*Overleaf: According to Feng Shui belief in the five elements, water is part of the productive
cycle when it creates wood, and part of the destructive cycle when it puts out fire.*

Suggested Further Reading

Eitel, Ernest J., *Feng-Shui — The Science of Sacred Landscape in Old China*, California 1993

Feuchtwang, Stephen D. R., *An Anthropological Analysis of Chinese Geomancy*, Vithagna, Laos 1974

Lau, Kwan, *Feng Shui for Today*, New York 1996

Lip, Evelyn, *Chinese Geomancy*, Times Books International 1979

Needham, Joseph, *Science and Civilisation in China*, Cambridge 1956, 1959

Rossbach, Sarah, *Feng Shui*, London 1987

Skinner, Stephen, *The Living Earth Manual of Feng-Shui*, London 1982

Walters, Derek, *Feng Shui*, London 1988

Wong, Eva, *Feng-Shui*, London 1996

Illustration Notes

❧

All diagrams supplied courtesy of Morse Modaberi.

Page 9 Detail from *The Hall of A Chinese Merchant's House with a Man Holding a Bird Cage* by Tinqua. Courtesy of Christie's Images. **Page 10** *The Hall of A Chinese Merchant's House with a Man Holding a Bird Cage* by Tinqua. Courtesy of Christie's Images. **Pages 12-13** *In the Well of the Great Wave of Kanagawa* by Katsushika Hokusai. Courtesy of Christie's Images. **Page 15** *Dragon and Tiger*. Courtesy of Circa Photo Library. **Pages 18-9** *A Six Leaf Screen*. Courtesy of Christie's Images. **Page 21** Detail from *Dragon and Tiger*. Courtesy of Circa Photo Library. **Pages 22-3** *Cosmic Turtle, Forbidden City, Beijing*. Courtesy of Circa Photo Library. **Page 24** *Magnificent Mountain Cottage in the Evening* by Pu Ru. Courtesy of Christie's Images. **Page 26** *Rare Massive Imperial Cloisonne Enamel Double-Gourd Plaque*. Courtesy of Christie's Images. **Page 29** *One of Two Hardstone-Mounted Lacquer Screens - With a Scholar Seated on an Elaborate Rock*. Courtesy of Christie's Images. **Page 31** *Hong Kong Quing Ming*. Courtesy of Circa Photo Library. **Pages 34-5** *Dragon Wall Carving, China*. Courtesy of Circa Photo Library. **Page 39** *Taoist Hanging Temple*. Courtesy of Circa Photo Library. **Pages 40-1** *Family Tomb*. Courtesy of Circa Photo Library. **Pages 50-1** *Hua Shan Taoist Mountain*. Courtesy of Circa Photo Library. **Page 61** *Chinese Geomancer's Compass*. Courtesy of the Science Museum/Science and Society Picture Library. **Pages 62-3** *The Hall of A Chinese Merchant's House with a Man Holding a Bird Cage* by Tinqua. Courtesy of Christie's Images. **Page 64** *Geomancer's Ruler* by Evelyn Lip. Courtesy of Times Books International. **Page 65** *Chinese Ba-Gua Mirror*. Courtesy of Circa Photo Library. **Pages 66-7** *Lake and a Bridge* by the Tinquai Studio. Courtesy of Christie's Images. **Page 69** *Magnificent Mountain Cottage in the Evening* by Pu Ru. Courtesy of Christie's Images. **Pages 70-1** Detail from *Lake and a Bridge* by the Tinquai Studio. Courtesy of Christie's Images. **Page 73** Detail from *The Hall of A Chinese Merchant's House with a Man Holding a Bird Cage* by Tinqua. Courtesy of Christie's Images. **Pages 76-7** Detail from *The Hall of A Chinese Merchant's House with a Man Holding a Bird Cage* by Tinqua. Courtesy of Christie's Images. **Page 78** *The Hong Kong and Shanghai Bank*. Courtesy of the Hongkong and Shanghai Banking Corporation. **Page 83** Detail from *Lake and a Bridge* by the Tinquai Studio. Courtesy of Christie's Images. **Pages 84-5** *A River Landscape with a Windmill* by Jacobus Maris. Courtesy of Christie's Images. **Page 87** *Large Mottled Jadeite Figure of a Guanyin*. Courtesy of Christie's Images. **Pages 88-9** *In the Well of the Great Wave of Kanagawa* by Katsushika Hokusai. Courtesy of Christie's Images.

Index

꩜

Index

❧